EKIBEN

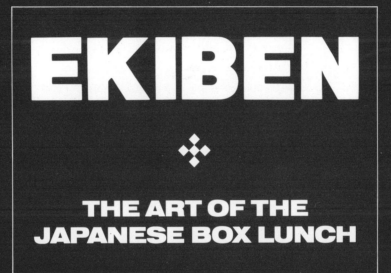

THE ART OF THE JAPANESE BOX LUNCH

JUNICHI KAMEKURA

MAMORU WATANABE

GIDEON BOSKER

CHRONICLE BOOKS ● SAN FRANCISCO

Printed in Korea

Library of Congress Cataloging in Publication Data:

Kamekura, Junichi
Ekiben: the art of the Japanese box lunch/ Junichi Kamekura, Mamoru Watanabe, Gideon Bosker.
    p.   cm.
ISBN 0-87701-490-6
1. Ekiben. 2. Convenience foods—Japan. 3. Convenience foods—Japan—Packaging. 4. Cookery, Japanese. I. Watanabe, Mamoru. II. Bosker, Gideon. III. Title. Tx724.5.J3K2OG 1989
847.9552—dc20   89-312TB
                                        CIP

Book and cover design: Takaaki Mizuno, TAXI, Tokyo.
Special thanks: Hiroki Akazaki
On the cover: Masu No Sushi
On the back cover: Gobou Makunouchi

Distributed in Canada by Raincoast Books, 112 East Third Avenue, Vancouver, B.C. V5T 1C8

10 9 8 7 6 5 4 3 2 1

Chronicle Books
275 Fifth Street
San Francisco, California 94103

CONTENTS

The sight is both familiar and exotic. Each day, millions of commuters clamber aboard the superexpress Tokaido Shinkansen, which connects Tokyo and Osaka with trains that whisk across the countryside at more than 140 miles per hour. As the gleaming metallic bullet slices full throttle through the verdant valleys and hillocks of the world's most productive industrial corridor, thousands of cross-country travelers nestle comfortably in plush velvet seats. Framed by sweeping panes of glass, they take in the scenery while quietly feasting on what some have called the finest and most sophisticated "fast food" in the world. Only a few moments before boarding these streamlined passenger cars, hordes of businessmen and vacationers assembled in cavernous train stations throughout the country. There, in what for more than a century has been an appetizing ritual of travel, they stopped at kiosks or flagged down roaming station vendors to purchase magical little food boxes known as ekiben.

Eki means "station," ben is short for *"bento,"* a ready-made meal packed in a container. As much as any other cultural factor, it is the development of Japan's highly efficient railway network that has given birth to this unique culinary phenomenon. Sold aboard trains and at railway stations across the country, ekiben is best described as "fast food" elevated to high art. If in the West the label "fast food" conjures up images of uniformly drab, mass-produced, and uninspired menus, in Japan ekiben stands for foods with a vibrantly regional inflection, dished up with wildly inventive local color. Ranging in price from three to eight dollars, depending upon ingredients, each ekiben is stylistically and gastronomically unique and reflects an innovative melding of indigenous culinary methods and fresh ingredients. Because every ekiben is pegged to some regional specialty, each train station is known for its unique variety of box lunch. In fact, this gastronomic package is so popular that Japan Railway (JR) annually publishes an inexpensive black-and-white ekiben guidebook listing the names and ingredients of box lunches featured at train stations across the country. Aficionados have been known to plan their travels around the shifting schedule of the ekiben, postponing trips until the agricultural calendar should once again turn propitious for a particular specialty.

Today, ekiben is to the urgently paced and omnipresent world of Japanese train culture what Kentucky Fried Chicken, A&W Root Beer, and McDonald's are to the gulp-it-as-you-run world of the American drive-in restaurant. For its respective nation and preferred mode of transportation, each style is a preeminent symbol of gastronomy on the go. Despite some similarities, however, there are important differences in the way these cultures produce and present fast food for mass consumption. For example, the eclectic, visually provocative and highly imaginative containers used in ekiben depart dramatically from the monotonous, predictable, and standardized package design that characterizes fast food in the United States. Whereas American fast food ethos stresses uniformity of ingredients across geographical boundaries, ekiben is distinguished by the fact that each box features a culinary distillate of the finest local foods available during a particular season. Given these differences, it is not surprising that over sixteen hundred ekiben varieties are available in Japan, with an estimated twelve million boxes sold daily at the nation's train stations.

In the topsy-turvy world of Japanese fast food, ekiben has become the most

conspicuous vehicle for expressing the culture's traditionally fertile culinary imagination and the fine art of gastronomic packaging for the masses. Although modern-day ekiben reflects sophisticated design trends and diverse culinary styles, its origins can be traced to the humble rice ball sold at the Utsunomiya Station in 1885. Wrapped in a single bamboo leaf, this progenitor of ekiben consisted of two rice balls packed around a center of pickled plums and sprinkled with a dusting of sesame salt.

Contemporary ekiben containers run the gamut from minimalist to witty. Within the boxes, several courses of a meal are typically accommodated. Sometimes the arrangement is sublime, understated, verging on the abstract. Sometimes, as in ekiben featuring such exotic comestibles as salmon roe, sea urchin, and chicken *shigure,* the culinary architecture is cubistic. The "variety" box lunch, *makunouchi bento,* may feature a regimented, crisply geometric display with a carefully balanced color scheme; in contrast, the *kamameshi bento,* employs porcelain pots filled with cooked rice topped with an accent scattering of assorted ingredients. At the wacky extreme are boxes fashioned in the shape of folding fans, tennis rackets, baseballs, and other artifacts that are symbolic of recreational activities integral to contemporary Japanese life.

Unlike American fast-food packaging, which relies almost exclusively on paper and plastic, ekiben draws upon a wealth of traditional and contemporary materials to make an explicit artistic statement. Most popular among these are bamboo, plastic, paper mesh, foil, leaves, and wood, all elegantly crafted to make a sculptural statement. When combined with such brightly pigmented ingredients as *echizen* crab, salmon roe, or *kinshi tamago,* the final effect is oftentimes theatrical and inspiring. Few will disagree that against the hustle-bustle of everyday life, the

Japanese businessman or student who rides the rails has access to an alluring, regionally specific collage of comestibles and containers that is guaranteed to please both the eye and the palate. For the tourist, this concession comes as a particular boon, offering a dual journey of discovery that lays bare the country's topography and the most representative aspects of its culinary legacy.

Fortunately, there is no such thing as a boilerplate design for ekiben. As is the case with so many aspects of Japanese cuisine, when it comes to fast food, variety—both visual and culinary—is the spice of life. For example, the exterior packaging may be quietist, simple, and neutral, while the contents may explode in a counterpoint of retina-searing arrangements. In the case of lunch boxes decorated with meticulously painted scenes of tranquil rivulets debouching into moonlit bays or of traditional watercolors depicting mackerel and tuna, the exterior wrapping can advertise important qualities of the region from which the food originates.

Although there is no formal scheme for categorizing ekiben, most boxes can readily be grouped according to packaging techniques and methods of food preparation. Novelty ekiben, for example, are recognized primarily by the shapes of their containers. Train stations that service resort areas with golf courses and tennis courts feature containers shaped like golf balls or tennis rackets. Upscale, or so-called gourmet, varieties feature brightly painted boxes in which each course of the meal is carefully assembled in two or three stacked layers.

Some ekiben varieties reflect seasonal changes in the availability of fresh ingredients. For instance, *Tako-meshi* ekiben is sold at Mihara Station only from May through October, when octopus is in season. In late fall, the ekiben distributed at this station features *matsutake* mushroom rice; during the winter, oyster rice is the signature preparation. Sushi also plays an important role in the ekiben culinary tradition. The possibilities range from hand-shaped *nigiri-sushi* to

chirashi-sushi and *oshi-sushi.*

Perhaps because of its extraordinarily diverse bill of fare and intriguing packaging, ekiben has become a gastronomic institution in which the Japanese take great pride. More than any other popular culinary movement, ekiben is a testimonial to the fact that food for the masses can be fashioned with elegance, wit, and grace.

EKIBEN

EKIBEN

NOVELTY EKIBEN

MOMOTARO NO MATSURI SUSHI

Sanyo Shinkansen Okayama Station

The idea for this ekiben dates back about four hundred years, to when Mitsumasa Ikeda, the feudal lord of the time, forbade any extravaganzas during festivals. As an alternative entertainment people made gorgeous *chirashi-sushi* for visitors. Soon the dish became a main attraction of the festivities. This *matsuri* ("festival") *bento* features just such a *chirashi-sushi*, which has become increasingly intricate over the years.

CHOCHIN BENTO
Tokaido Shinkansen Odawara Station

Odawara, a city in Kanagawa Prefecture, is renowned for its elastic paper lanterns *("chochin")*, the inspirations for this container. The ekiben features lightly flavored rice topped with grilled eel.

KISHU TEMARI BENTO
Kisei Honsen Kii Tanabe Station

Formed into the shape of *temari*, or "handball," this ekiben from Kishu Prefecture contains rice cooked in chicken stock topped with local vegetables and seafood. The container can be kept and used as a piggy bank.

TANABATA KOKESHIKKO
Tohoku Shinkansen Sendai Station

Tanabata is a festival held every July 7, a day when young girls write their wishes on paper strips and hang them from bamboo branches. Sendai city of Miyagi Prefecture is known for its particularly elaborate *Tanabata* celebration. *Kokeshi*, a wooden doll, is the most popular souvenir of the area. This ekiben, which joins the two names in order to intensify the local connection, presents chicken teriyaki, *kamaboko* with plum flavor, and boiled chestnuts on rice in a ceramic container.

GORUFU BENTO
Shinetsu Honsen Karuizawa Station

Karuizawa of Nagano Prefecture is one of the most popular resort areas of Japan. Golf, tennis, and cycling are a few of the recreations that can be enjoyed there. This truly kitsch ekiben container holds western-style pilaf topped with fried shrimp and sausages.

TENISU BENTO

Shinetsu Honsen Karuizawa Station

Another ekiben of Karuizawa, this box features lightly flavored rice topped with panfried beef and *kinshi-tamago* packed into a container shaped like a tennis racquet.

ECHIZEN KANI-MESHI
Hokuriku Honsen Fukui Station

Echizen crab, also known as *"zuwai"* or "snow crab," is the primary ingredient in this box. The male crab stretches seventy centimeters from the tip of the right to the tip of the left leg. The eggs, ovaries, and internal organs of the female crab (a bit smaller than the male) are cooked with rice and topped with the meat of the male.

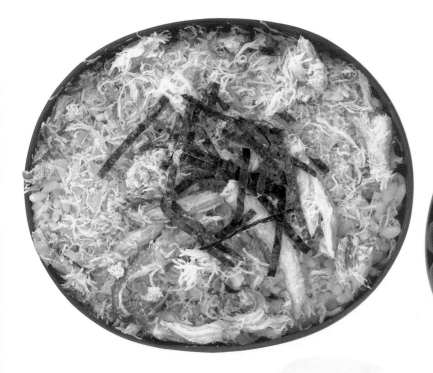

SHAMOJI KAKI-MESHI
Sanyo Shinkansen Hiroshima Station

Hiroshima Prefecture produces seventy to eighty percent of Japan's oysters ("*kaki*"). This ekiben is an "oyster-on-parade," showcasing the mollusk as fried oysters, boiled oysters, and rice cooked with oysters. *Shamoji* is the term for a wooden spoon or ladle.

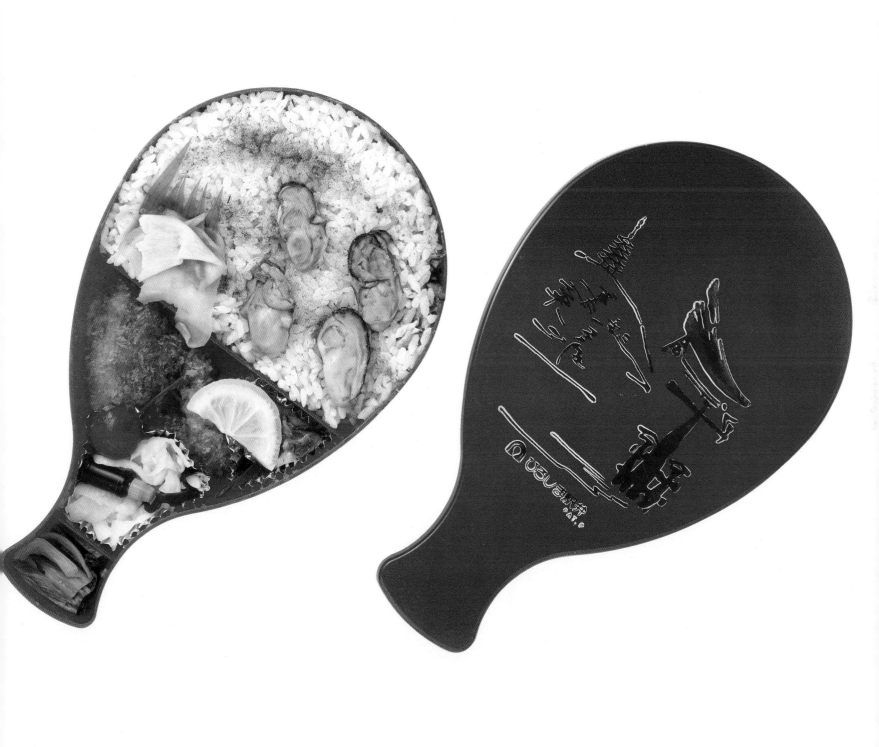

OKAME BENTO

Sanyo Shinkansen Himeji Station

Okame ("moon-faced") was a term commonly used to describe Japanese women during the Edo period. This box features rice flavored with tuna stock and topped with *kinshi-tamago*, boiled shrimp, octopus, conger eel, and squid. The picture of the *okame* on the outer cover can be cut out and used as a mask.

おかめ弁当

＊お面のつくり方＊

(1)
お面の目の部分
を点線にそって
あけてください

(2)
左右の耳の部分に弁当の
輪ゴムを図のように取付
けます

輪ゴム

(3)
楽しいお面の出来上り

DARUMA BENTO
Joetsu Shinkansen Takasaki Station

The visual concept for this *bento* is the blank-eyed *daruma* doll, a good-luck figure sold at the *Daruma* Market held every New Year in the city of Takasaki. The buyer draws in one eye while making a wish; the other eye is added when the wish comes true. The container can be saved to use as a piggy bank.

KURI OKOWA
Sanyo Shinkansen Okayama Station

Okayama Prefecture is known for its chestnuts. Here, fresh mountain-grown *kuri* ("chestnuts") come with *okowa* in a container shaped like the nut.

HOTATE FUKI-YOSE
Seikan Renrakusen

Although the term ekiben most often refers to the box lunch found at train stations, this one was originally sold on the ship that connected Aomori Prefecture, located on Honshu, with Hokkaido. With the opening of the Seikan Tunnel on March 13, 1988, the water route was discontinued. The ekiben was also on the chopping block, but because of its popularity, production continues. *Hotate fuki-yose* combines scallops (*hotate*) from Funka Bay on the southwest coast of Hokkaido, with squid, herring, and salmon, and serves them atop lightly seasoned rice.

SUSHI EKIBEN

MASU NO SUSHI

Hokuriku Honsen Toyama Station

Nicknamed the Grand Champion of Western Japan, this very popular eki-ben featuring *oshi-sushi* draws its inspiration from the *nare-sushi* of the Heian period thirteen hundred years ago. During that era, fish and other seafood were first preserved in salt and then fermented with the addition of rice. Vinegar-flavored rice was adopted in the late Edo period, a change that led to today's *chirashi-sushi* and *nigiri-sushi*. The fish used in this bento is *masu,* a type of river trout.

KIYOHIME NO ICHIYA SUSHI
Kisei Honsen Gobou Station

According to legend, there was once a monk named Anjin who fell in love with Kiyohime, the daughter of a merchant. One day Anjin decided to leave Kiyohime and never return from his journey. The poor, distraught Kiyohime followed him. Even though Anjin had deserted her, Kiyohime was merciful enough to bring him what she thought was the most delicious of all foods, the *nare-sushi* of Kishu. This ekiben owes its name to that touching love story. Local mackerel is salted and pressed for one night and then wrapped in bamboo leaf with rice; this type of pressed sushi is called *ichiya-sushi*.

KODAI SUZUME

Kisei Honsen Wakayama Station

Kodai ("small sea bream"), found in the waters near Katamachi in Wa-kayama Prefecture, is prepared as *nigiri-sushi* for this ekiben. The meat is firm and especially delicate.

SANMA SUSHI

Kisei Honsen Kumano Station

Sanma (mackerel pikes or saurys) are generally said to taste best in autumn, but those used in this lunch box are caught in December, when they have shed their fat from swimming south in cold winter currents and are at their optimum for sushi. The fish are first soaked in salt, then marinated in vinegar and citron, and served as *oshi-sushi* wrapped in seaweed. In the Kumano area, *sanma sushi* is included as a delicacy in the New Year's feast.

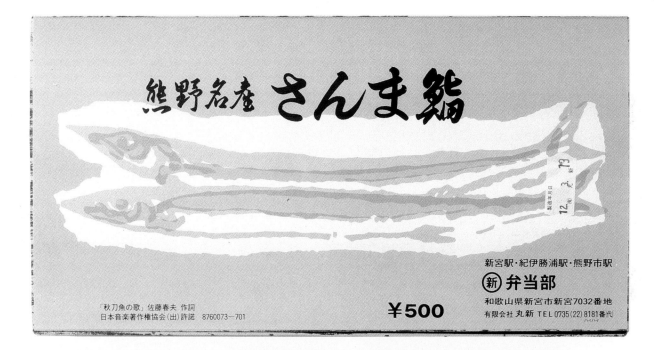

AYU SUSHI
Tokaido Shinkansen Gifu Station

This ekiben from Gifu Prefecture contains what is recognized as the "original" *ayu sushi*. It is a dish that is known to have been prepared thirteen hundred years ago in the Heian period, and some two hundred years ago, in the Edo era, it was regularly being served to the shogun. For this lunch box, the *ayu* is caught in the Nagara River and the rice is locally grown. The accompaniments are pickled ginger and *sansho*, a tangy spice made from the pod of the prickly ash.

YAMAME SUSHI
Tokaido Shinkansen Hamamatsu Station

Yamame, members of the salmon family, are found in the fresh waters of northern Japan. Because they are difficult to catch, the *yamame* used in this ekiben are artificially grown in Shizuoka Prefecture and then prepared as *oshi-sushi.*

MAMAKARI SUSHI

Sanyo Shinkansen Fukuyama Station

About ten centimeters in length, *mamakari* is a small fish similar to the sardine. *Mama* means *"rice"* and *kari* means "burrow." It is said that the fish are so good, you would even burrow into your neighbor's rice to taste them. In this ekiben, *mamakari* is marinated in vinegar and served as *nigiri-sushi*.

MASU NO SUSHI
Sanyo Shinkansen Ogori Station

Here, *masu*, a local rainbow trout, is served as sushi. First, the trout's stomach is slit open and the bones and internal organs are removed. Then, the boned whole fish is marinated in vinegar and stuffed with vinegared rice. Trout has less calories than beef or chicken, and is high in calcium, protein, and vitamin A. This is a simple, but nutritious ekiben.

UKAI CHIRASHI
Tokaido Shinkansen Gifu Station

Developed by a man named Usho, *ukai* refers to a thousand-year-old method of catching a type of river trout called *ayu*. Usho tied a rope to a wild duck that he trained to first swallow and then disgorge the fish. In the summertime, one can still see tethered ducks bobbing for fish on the Nagara River in Gifu Prefecture. *Ukai chirashi,* which is derived from this traditional event, features sliced *ayu*, broiled eel, crab, *shiitake* mushrooms, and *kinshi-tamago* atop vinegared rice. It comes in a package with a drawing of Usho aboard a *ukai* boat.

MUTSUGORO CHIRASHI SUSHI

Nagasaki Honsen Hizen Yamaguchi Station

A relative of the goby, *mutsugoro* ("mudskipper") is found in the Ariake Sea of western Kyushu. It has huge eyes and looks a bit grotesque, but is very tasty. *Mutsugoro* boiled in soy sauce, *kinshi-tamago*, and *shiitake* mushrooms are arranged over rice for this *chirashi-sushi*.

NUKU-SUSHI
Sanyo Shinkansen Okayama Station

Nuku-sushi is warm *chirashi-sushi*, a style popular along the coast of Okayama Prefecture, where it is often served at weddings. In order to keep the ekiben warm, a disposable pocket warmer that heats for nine hours is inserted beneath the lunch box, which is then wrapped with aluminum foil.

KAKI NO HA SUSHI
Wakayama Sen Yoshinoguchi Station

Nara Prefecture is known for its *kaki* ("persimmons"). The persimmon leaves used in this ekiben are picked in May or June when they are still astringent. Mackerel from Wakayama Prefecture is sliced and placed on vinegar-flavored rice, which is then wrapped in persimmon leaves, pressed, and left overnight. The leaves, which have an aroma similar to that of cherry leaves, eliminate the mackerel's fishy smell and soften the rice.

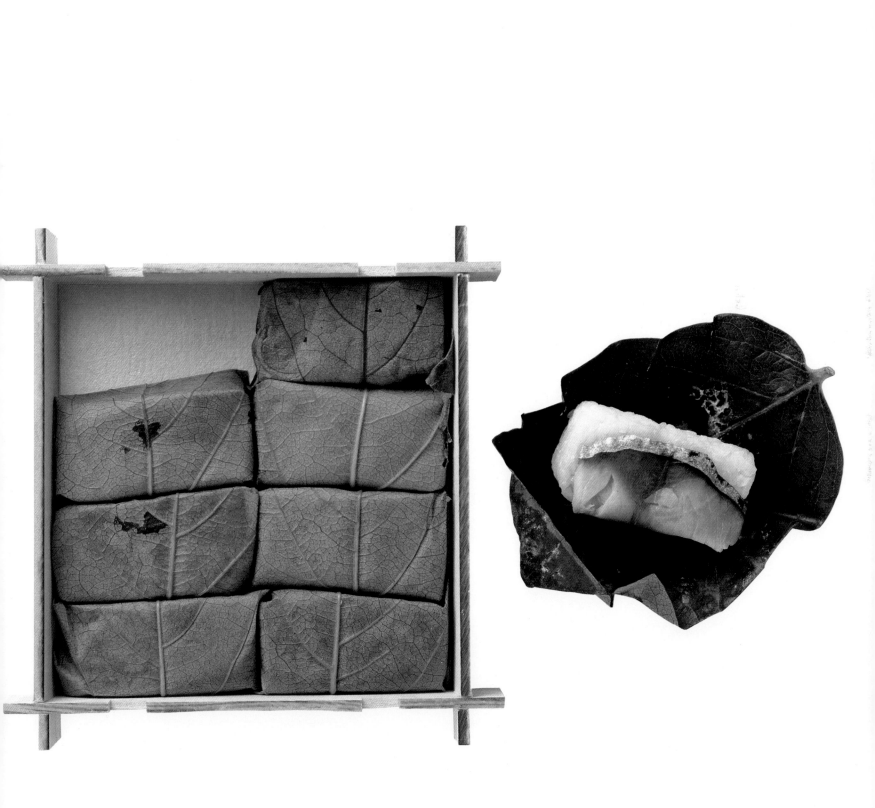

YAMABE SHAKE SUSHI
Hakodate Honsen Sapporo Station

Yamame (salmon) is known as "*yamabe*" in Sapporo. *Yamabe* and red salmon are marinated in sweet vinegar and served as *oshi-sushi* in a box made from the wood of the *todo* pine tree. The mild aroma of *yamabe* mingled with pine whets the appetite. This ekiben was first made during the Sapporo Winter Olympics.

EBI SUSHI
Tokaido Shinkansen Shizuoka Station

Boiled shrimp are neatly arranged on vinegar-flavored rice and served as *oshi-sushi*. This simple box lunch has a perfectly balanced flavor.

SETO NO HANA SUSHI

Sanyo Shinkansen Shin-Kobe Station

On April 1, 1987, Japan National Railway became a private corporation and was named Japan Railway, or JR. This ekiben was created to commemorate the new JR Western Japan and the one hundred twentieth anniversary of the port of Kobe. It features red snapper and thread herring from the Inland Sea, and red salmon and herring roe from Hokkaido. The fish is prepared in *oshi-sushi* style, using locally grown rice. The flavor is sweet and delicate.

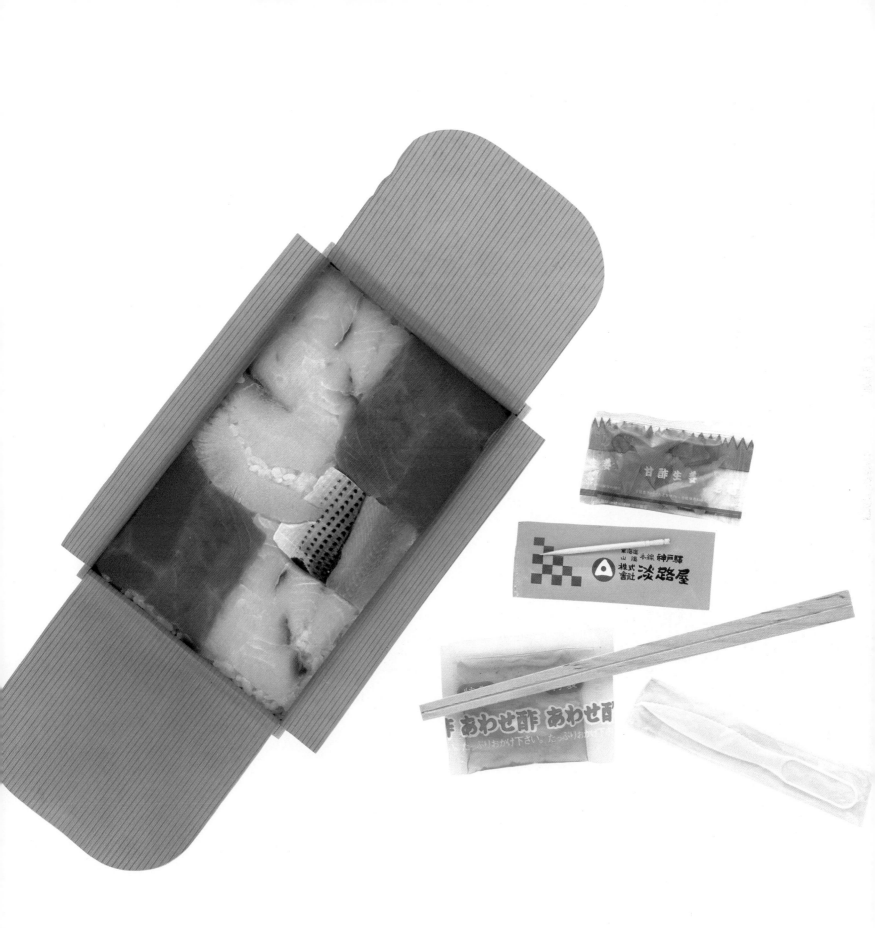

SABA BOU SUSHI

Kansai Honsen Tennoji Station

This ekiben features *saba* ("mackerel") caught in the waters neighboring Tennoji. The fish is first marinated in salt and vinegar, then wrapped in a special seaweed that makes the flesh especially mild and tender. Finally, it is encased in bamboo leaf and left for one day. The taste improves when the mackerel rests untouched for an additional twenty-four hours.

BANDAI SASA SUSHI
Tohoku Shinkansen Koriyama Station

Salmon and sea bream are wrapped in *sasa* ("bamboo leaf") with rice and served as sushi. This ekiben is thought of as "preservation food," because it keeps for a long time; some people even bring the box home instead of eating it on the train.

CHIMAKI SUSHI

Sanyo Shinkansen Mihara Station

Chimaki sushi, a form of *nare-sushi,* is a traditional delicacy of Mihara, a town in Hiroshima Prefecture. It features cooked flounder, salmon, and shrimp wrapped together with vinegar-flavored rice, and tastes best when eaten twenty-four hours after preparation.

65

OSAKA SUSHI
Kansai Honsen Tennoji Station

Nigiri-sushi originated in the Kanto region, around Tokyo, while *oshi-sushi* was developed in the Kansai area, around Osaka. This popular Osaka ekiben features both *oshi-sushi* and *maki-sushi*. In Kansai, more sugar is added to the rice and the fish is lightly flavored, so the sushi keeps better, making it more suitable than the Kanto style for box lunches.

大阪寿司

¥800

有限
会社 芦の家

MOMIJI NO SATO

Tokaido Honsen Mihara Station

This *maki-sushi* contains broiled conger eel found in Mihara Bay, pickled cucumbers, trefoil, white sesame seeds, and seaweed boiled in soy sauce. The ekiben wrapper displays a picture of a *momiji* ("maple leaf"), which is the symbol of Hiroshima Prefecture.

GOZAEMON SUSHI

Sanin Honsen Yonago Station

Gozaemon sushi is a rolled sushi made of mackerel pulled from the Sea of Japan. First saturated with vinegar and drained, the fish is then wrapped in *chikuzen* seaweed from Hokkaido. The ekiben takes its name from Yoneya Gozaemon, a merchant whose wife made this box lunch for her family 350 years ago. Although this ekiben has been updated, it maintains tradition by having the sushi wrapped in bamboo leaf.

GORGEOUS GOURMET BENTO

HAMA GOZEN
Tokaido Shinkansen Shin-Yokohama Station

Hama Gozen, a two-tiered ekiben, is first tied with a red-and-white ceremonial rope and then wrapped in a cloth printed with flowers and turtles. The top layer has various foods, neatly arranged; the bottom layer holds rice in the shape of a folding fan, and *konomono.* The meal itself is traditionally served to accompany the tea ceremony.

浜御膳

崎陽軒

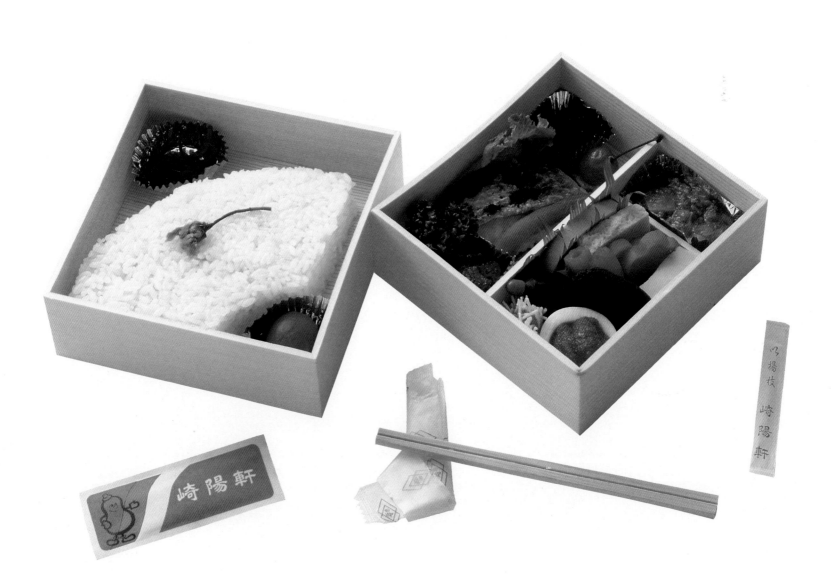

HANA KATAMI

Tokaido Shinkansen Shin-Yokohama Station

This container is quite extraordinary. An octagonal box resembling a folding fan is tied with a red-and-white ceremonial paper cord to which is fastened a *tanzaku* (paper strip on which Japanese poems are written) that reads "*Hana Katami*." A variety of foods such as *kinshi-tamago*, tuna *soboro*, salmon roe, and conger eel are beautifully arrayed on vinegar-flavored rice. The name *Hana katami*, which means "flower basket," comes from a song in a classical Japanese "Noh" drama.

NAGOYA ZANMAI

Tokaido Shinkansen Nagoya Station

The container for this three-layer ekiben, which has been sold for more than a century, is as deluxe as its contents. The bottom tier contains white rice and *sansai okowa* (mountain vegetables mixed into red-bean rice) shaped to resemble a pine leaf. The second layer holds chicken *soboro* topped with chicken and eggs. The top tier is full of locally harvested vegetables, seafood such as clams, and chicken *shigure*. The box is decorated with illustrations of Meiji Village, Tsushima Tennogawa Festival, and Nagoya Castle, all of which represent Aichi Prefecture.

SANSHOKU BENTO

Sanyo Shinkansen Hakata Station

Designing an ekiben in two or three tiers has recently become very popular. The *Sanshoku* ("Three-Color") *Bento* is actually a union of three different lunches. The black box contains rice in the shape of a gourd, shrimp, *kamaboko,* and *tamago-yaki,* made in *makunouchi* style. The red box has *kashiwa-meshi* (rice cooked with chicken) with additional chicken on top, *kinshi-tamago,* and a crown of dried seaweed. The green box is filled with *chirashi-sushi* topped with *shiitake* mushrooms, *kinshi-tamago,* and sea bream marinated in vinegar.

SANSHOKU BENTO YAGURA

Sanyo Shinkansen Himeji Station

Himeji Castle, also known as Shirasagi Castle, is one of the three most eminent castles of Japan, and is the inspiration for this ekiben. The three layers are arranged in a manner similar to that of the *Sanshoku Bento* described on the previous page, but the *yagura*, or "tower," has more seafood.

WAFU KASANE BENTO
Tohoku Shinkansen Koriyama Station

This elegant two-layered *makunouchi bento* was created to commemorate the building of the Tohoku Shinkansen Line. The bottom layer holds rice cooked with *sansai*, and the top, various delicacies. The box is decorated with drawings of local toys and their descriptions. Both the meal and the box are enjoyed during a trip on the train.

OHARA SHOSUKE BENTO
Tohoku Shinkansen Fukushima Station

A Fukushima folk song describes Ohara Shosuke as a very lazy character who enjoyed sleeping, drinking, and bathing in the morning. This ekiben, which bears his name, is divided into two layers. The box on the bottom contains rice cooked with five kinds of *sansai* and *nano hana*, topped with *shimeji* mushrooms. The top layer features fried shrimp wrapped in beefsteak leaf, burdock wrapped in chicken meat, and herring wrapped in seaweed.

TOOGE NO KAMA-MESHI

Shinetsu Honsen Yokokawa Station

Many Japanese consider the *kama-meshi* of Yokokawa the country's premier ekiben. Two brands of high-quality rice are cooked, lightly flavored, and then topped with chicken, *shiitake* mushrooms, burdock, and apricot. No preservative or artificial flavoring is added. This was the first ekiben to use a pottery container.

BANDAI KAMA-MESHI
Tohoku Shinkansen Koriyama Station

Chicken, two preparations of burdock, vinegared lotus stem, *shiitake* mushroom, chestnut, and boiled butterbur (a green vegetable) are arranged on flavored rice packed into an earthenware pot with wooden lid. The container can be saved and taken home to use for rice porridge or noodle soup.

ODORIKO BENTO
Tokaido Shinkansen Atami Station

This ekiben is named after Yasunari Kawabata's novel *Izu No Odoriko* ("Izu Dancer"). Twelve seasonal foods such as *wasabi-zuke* (pickled horseradish), burdock, *shiitake* mushrooms, bamboo shoots, eel, chicken *soboro*, and gingko nuts are packed into a container of Mino-yaki pottery. After devouring the contents, the box can be taken home and used as candy dish or a wall decoration.

HAMA NO KAMA-MESHI
Tokaido Shinkansen Hamamatsu Station

The lunch box contains three small broiled eel, *shiitake* mushrooms, white-fish fillet, and chicken *soboro*, nicely arranged on rice that has been flavored with soy sauce. It is very popular among families because it comes with a spoon, which makes is easier for children to eat.

TSUKIMI GOMOKU-MESHI
Shinoi Sen Matsumoto Station

Tucked away in the Japan Alps, the provincial town of Matsumoto is famous for its elegant sixteenth-century castle, complete with a *tsukimi yagura*, or "moon-watching tower," located on the rooftop. Many years ago, the master of the castle, Kazumasa Ishikawa, held banquets in the *tsukimi yagura* and served his guests game, which he called *Musha Ryori* ("Food of Warriors").

ONE-OF-A-KIND EKIBEN

EZO WAPPA

Hakodate Honsen Asahikawa Station

The city of Asahikawa, in central Hokkaido, is where seafoods from the Sea of Japan and the Sea of Ohotsuku meet the abundant harvests of the fertile inlands. This ekiben features a *wappa* preparation (rice with a variety of toppings), lightly flavored rice topped with *kinshi-tamago*, *nano hana*, and the muscular meat of scallops, boiled in soy sauce. It comes with salmon roe, sea urchin, or crab as the main dish.

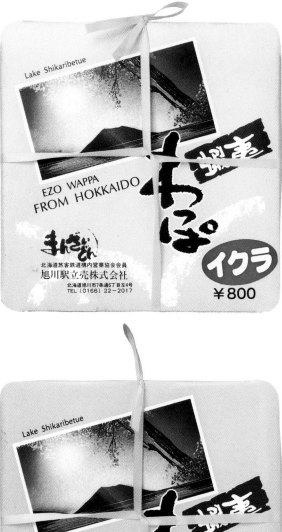

Lake Shikaribetue

WAPPA
OKKAIDO

IKA-MESHI
Hakodate Honsen Mori Station

At the many ekiben conventions held in department stores throughout Japan, *ika-meshi* ("squid rice") is often the most popular lunch box with the customers. It is even referred to as the Grand Champion of Eastern Japan. This box contains two types of rice, *mochi* (glutinous) and *uruchi* (nonglutinous) stuffed in summer squid and cooked in soup stock.

TAKO-MESHI
Sanyo Shinkansen Mihara Station

The label features a drawing of what looks like an octopus lying down on a jar. Actually, the picture illustrates how octopus are caught by trapping them in jars suspended into the water from ropes. This is the only ekiben in Japan that features octopus as its main dish; it is sold from May through October.

SHAKO-MESHI
Sanyo Shinkansen Aioi Station

Shako ("mantis shrimp") from the Inland Sea have a reputation for high quality; they are meaty and tasty. The rice is cooked with potato curd, carrot, burdock, and fried soybean paste, a local specialty. *Kinshi-tamago*, *shako*, shrimps and clams are then delicately placed on top.

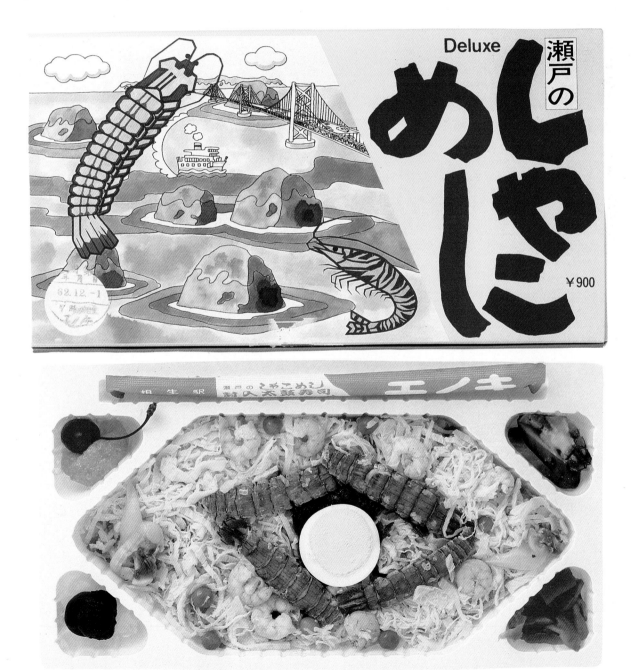

THE EKIBEN

Sanyo Shinkansen Mihara Station

The menu of this ekiben changes according to season. *Tako-meshi* ("octopus rice") in spring, *matsutake-meshi* ("*matsutake* mushroom rice") in autumn, *anago-meshi* ("conger eel rice") in summer, and *kaki-meshi* ("oyster rice") in winter.

AYU NO KABAYAKI BENTO

Nippo Honsen Nobeoka Station

For this ekiben, *ayu* is prepared in the classic manner for *kabayaki*, a type of eel. First, the larger bones of the fish are removed and discarded and the flesh is broiled. Then it is simmered for half a day, which eliminates much of the fat and tenderizes the meat. The rice, which has been cooked in stock made from the fish bones, is flavored with soy sauce.

IKURA BENTO
Hakodate Honsen Otaru Station

Seafood is abundant in the port city of Otaru, which is home to many excellent sushi bars. This ekiben contains salted salmon roe (*ikura*), herring roe, squid, *shiitake* mushrooms, and *kikurage* (cloud ear fungus), tossed together and attractively arranged on vinegared rice.

EKIBEN FOR ALL SEASONS

TORI-MESHI
Joetsu Shinkansen Takasaki Station

In Gunma Prefecture in the northern Kanto region lies the town of Takasaki, which is known for its delicious chickens. This lunch box is composed of chicken teriyaki, chicken *soboro*, and boiled chicken, each placed on top of rice that has been cooked in chicken stock.

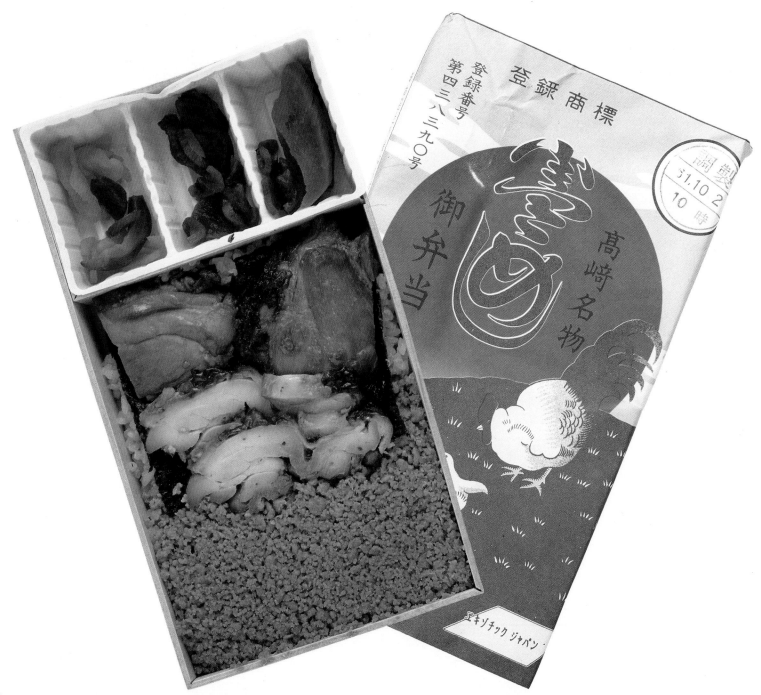

SHABU-SHABU BENTO MURASAME

Sanyo Shinkansen Shin-Kobe Station

Shabu-shabu is a cooking style in which the diners themselves prepare their meals by dipping meat into a pot of boiling water. The term is onomatopoeic, derived from the hissing sound the meat makes when it is immersed in the hot liquid. The top layer of the bento holds Kobe beef and vegetables on a bed of lettuce leaves; the bottom layer is rice and three different kinds of dressing, one for the lettuce and two others, vinegar and sesame, for the meat. *Shabu-shabu* is best when eaten warm, so the meal is cooked in a special manner that maintains the flavor even when the food is cool.

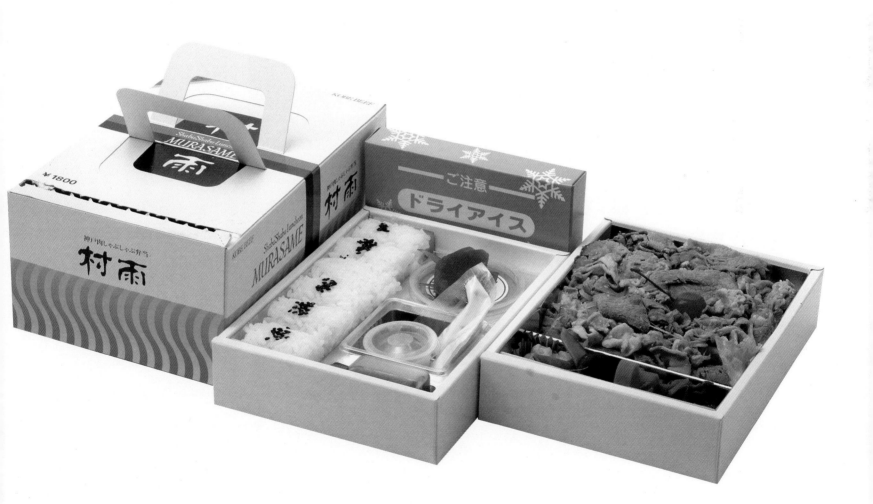

NIKU-MESHI
Sanyo Shinkansen Shin-Kobe Station

Kobe beef, known the world over as a premium meat, is the main ingredient of this ekiben. In order to prevent the kernels from hardening when the meat fat cools, the rice is cooked in beef stock. The topping is barbecued beef that is flavored with a dozen spices for seven hours before it is grilled. The dish also includes plum pickles wrapped in beefsteak leaves (which aid digestion), *narazuke* ("sweet pickles"), and pineapple for dessert.

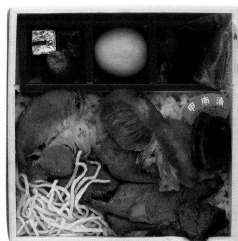

GANSO GYUNIKU BENTO
Kisei Honsen Matsusaka Station

The town of Matsusaka, in Mie Prefecture not far from Nagoya, is known for its high-quality meat, popularly called Matsusaka beef. The cattle are fed beer and then massaged with *shochu* (a type of inexpensive distilled spirits) to tenderize their flesh. In this ekiben, lean Matsusaka beef is saturated with red wine, basted with a semi-sweet sauce and then steamed.

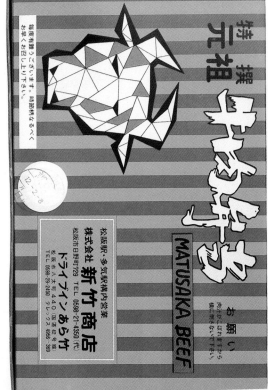

SANSAI KIJI-YAKI BENTO
Tohoku Shinkansen Koriyama Station

Kiji-Yaki, a technique for broiling sauce-basted fish, meats, or vegetables, is usually reserved for special occasions. In this lunch box, chicken prepared *kiji-yaki* style is topped with extra sauce, boiled bamboo shoots, and *shiitake* mushrooms. Pickled eggplants laced with hot pepper, burdock preserved in *miso* (fermented soybean paste), and other local vegetables are also included in the *bento.*

OUTRAGEOUS EKIBEN

KOHOKU NO OHANASHI

Tokaido Shinkansen Maibara Station

Duck roasted with pepper is featured in this lunch box, which also includes such seasonal side dishes as *okowa,* country-style potato curd flavored hot and sweet, and sautéed small whole potatoes.

湖北のおはなし

一、金九百円也
正に領収仕り候

まいばら いづつや

CHA-MESHI
Tokaido Shinkansen Shizuoka Station

This box is characteristic of Shizuoka Prefecture, which is famous for its tea. The rice is cooked in high-quality tea and served with fried shrimp, broiled chicken thighs, and fish teriyaki; fresh tea leaves are used for the garnish.

GENMAI BENTO
Shinetsu Honsen Yokokawa Station

There is no white rice, white sugar, preservatives, or artificial flavorings in this *bento*. The *genmai* ("unpolished rice") is cooked with pearl barley and red beans in a pressure cooker.

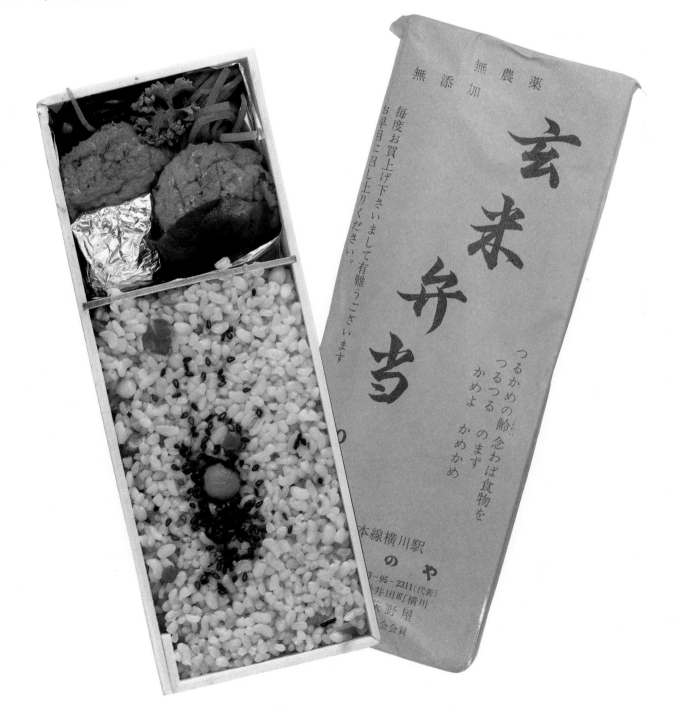

無農薬
無添加

玄米弁当

毎度お買上げ下さいまして有難うございます
お早目に召し上りください。

つるかめの齢念わば食物を
つるつる のまず
かめよ かめかめ

本線横川駅
のや
8—95—2311(代表)
井田町横川
永野屋
会会員

KIKU-SHU BENTO
Hokuriku Honsen Kanazawa Station

This unique ekiben includes two small bottles of sake, one sweet and one dry. It contains various ingredients, including *kamaboko*, shrimp, and sea urchin, all of which are enhanced by the flavor of sake.

SL BENTO
Hakodate Honsen Sapporo Station

SL stands for "Steam Locomotive"; this ekiben was named in honor of the 1980 Hokkaido Railroad centennial. The lunch box, which is divided into four sections that resemble train windows, is equipped with edible wheels made out of dried seaweed. Salmon, herring, boiled vegetables, and many other Hokkaido specialties are also included.

KISHU "TONO-SAMA" BENTO
Kisei Honsen Kii Tanabe Station

This ekiben brings together such diverse ingredients as red snapper *oshi-sushi*, *tamago-yaki*, marinated short-necked clams and sea urchins, Chinese-style chicken, hamburger (without the bun), and *gobou-maki* (rolled burdock). The term *"tono-sama"* was used for lords in feudal Japan.

おてもと

南紀白浜温泉白浜
南紀白浜駅構内営業
紀伊田辺駅

駅弁 あしべ

〒646 和歌山県田辺市湊943
電話 0739-24-6363㈹
テレックス 5562-109

SASA-MAKI OKOWA
Joetsu Shinkansen Niigata Station

In Japan, May 5 is the national holiday called *Tango no Sekku*, or "Boys' Day." Every year on this date, a boy's future is celebrated by outfitting him with irises, armor, helmet, and sword, and by eating *chimaki*, *okowa* and chestnuts enclosed in *sasa* ("bamboo leaf").

YAMATO NO CHAGAYU

Kansai Honsen Nara Station

Yamato street, in the town of Nara, ranks with parts of Kyoto in historical importance. Many traditional foods are still found along this street, and *chagayu* ("rice porridge") is one of them. The porridge in this bento is cooked with bancha, a common Japanese tea, and is served with white rice, *ume-boshi* ("pickled plums"), and *konomono*.

GLOSSARY

Ayu
A type of river trout sweetfish

Bento
Japanese-style box lunch

Burdock
Long, slender root vegetable

Chirashi-sushi
Sushi that is not shaped with the fingers, but rather rice put into a bowl and topped with seafood and vegetables.

Kamaboko
Fish cake

Kinshi-tamago
"Golden strings"; very finely shredded omelet

Konomono
Pickled vegetables

Kama-meshi
Seasoned rice topped with meats or seafood and vegetables cooked together in a ceramic pot.

Maki-sushi
"Rolled sushi" vegetables and/or fish arranged on a layer of rice, which is then rolled into a cylinder encased in a seaweed wrapper.

Makunouchi bento
Box lunch containing a variety of foods

Masu
A local variety of river trout

Matsutake mushroom
Deep brown mushroom with a thick stem that grows wild in pine forests

Nano hana
Rape blossoms

Nare-sushi
A thirteen-hundred-year-old method of pickling foods by packing them between layers of cooked rice, which then ferments

Nigiri-sushi
"Caked sushi," i.e., rice pressed into shape by hand; the ovals of rice are then topped with fish

Okowa
Steamed glutinous rice mixed with red beans

Oshi-sushi
So-called pressed sushi, made by pressing fish and rice in a container rather than shaping by hand

Prefecture
The term used for a regional unit of government in Japan

Sansai
Mountain-grown vegetables

Sasa
Bamboo leaf

Shigure
Simmered in soy sauce

Shiitake mushroom
Dark brown mushroom with a large, thick cap

Shimeji mushroom
Champignon

Soboro
Seasoned crumbled meats or fish

Tamago-yaki
Fried-egg cake

Yamame
A local variety of river trout